MICROPRODUCTIVIT Y IN 15 MINUTES

The Tiny Habit That Will Lead You To Huge Wins

by Ivan Kuznietsov

COPYRIGHT AND DISCLAIMERS

Microproductivity in 15 Minutes
by Ivan Kuznietsov

The author reserves the right to make any changes he deems necessary to future versions of the publication to ensure its accuracy.

ABOUT THE AUTHOR

Ivan Kuznietsov is a certified Agile Coach and international author focused on habits and continuous improvement. He is known for delivering highly actionable, world-class behavior change strategies for teams and individuals. Ivan writes books with one simple aim in mind: to teach people new micro habits in 15 minutes a day.

Ivan was born in Ukraine, but currently he lives and works in Vienna, Austria.

DEDICATION

To my family who supports me to explore.

EPIGRAPH

micro

- extremely small in scale or scope

habit

- a routine or practice performed regularly

productivity

- the quality of being productive or having the power to produce

PREFACE

I had experimented with personal development strategies for a decade. When I accidentally started my first micro habit in 2018—and the changes I made were actually lasting—I realized the prior techniques I relied on were complete failures. But the truth is the problem wasn't with them, it was with my approach to them.

The science in Micro Habits book series exposes the most popular personal growth strategies as predictably inconsistent and shows why micro habits are the most effective and reliable way to live a happy and productive life.

When you start reading Micro Habits, and then again after you start your first micro habit, you'll wonder why nobody told you about this strategy before, and where it's been all your life. Well, nobody told me either. But let's focus on your bright future because micro habits will surprisingly change your life.

ABOUT MICRO HABITS BOOK SERIES

Micro Habits can change your life in 15 minutes a day!

Dreaming big is important, but often, big goals start with micro-steps. Bite-size, low-time-commitment habits can help you gradually achieve your goals in doable steps. Just a few minutes a day can lay the foundation you need to make your big dreams come true.

What are Micro Habits?

Micro habits are tiny, everyday habits that steer you toward big results. Because they are too small and not time-consuming, they are easy to incorporate into your daily life. If you've ever made New Year's resolutions, you know how hard they can be to see through. But micro habits aren't daunting—rather, they're quick wins to keep you motivated.

Here are a few ways micro shifts lead to lasting change:

- Micro habits can help to break bad habits.
- Tiny life changes make it easier to implement new, productive habits.
- The adjustments feel natural over time and eventually become a normal part of your character and routine.

Micro habits are easy, small changes that lead to big shifts in your health, finances, and personal growth. If you are ready to improve your life, in the Micro Habits book series you will find the most useful micro habits to try, whether your goals are to get fit, be more creative, or just improve the quality of your life. Get started on micro habits today and notice how they keep you motivated over time.

ABOUT MICROPRODUCTIVITY IN 15 MINUTES BOOK

A certified Agile Coach shares his breakthrough method for increasing productivity quickly and easily. With *Microproductivity in 15 Minutes* you'll increase productivity by tapping into positive emotions to create a happier and healthier life.

"There are many great books on the topic [of productivity], but this offers the most simple, practical, and compassionate method I've ever come across." — Roger Ebert, Goodreads user

Ivan is here to change your life—and revolutionize how we think about human productivity. Based on ten years of experience coaching production teams, *Microproductivity in 15 Minutes* cracks the code of productivity habits formation. With breakthrough discoveries in every chapter, you'll learn the simplest proven ways to transform your life. Ivan shows you how to feel good about your small successes instead of waiting for better days. Whether you want to be more productive at work or home, *Microproductivity in 15 Minutes* makes it easy to achieve—by starting micro.

CONTENTS

THE ONLY WAY
TO ASSEMBLE
A BIG PUZZLE

"When assembling a puzzle, take one piece at a time."

How we set our goals has everything to do with whether or not we achieve them. One wise man said, "there is only one way to assemble a large puzzle: a piece at a time." What he meant by this is that everything in life that seems daunting, overwhelming, and even impossible can be accomplished gradually by taking on just a little step at a time.

If you've ever wanted to accomplish something major, you know that getting started can be a bit of a challenge. Maybe you have some vague idea about what you want but no clue how to get it. Or perhaps you sit down to think about everything you have to do and get completely intimidated, freezing up and feeling incapable of taking the first step.

This is a common experience, and it's the reason so many people fall short of turning their dreams into reality. They try to assemble the whole puzzle in a single moment.

One very important key to assembling a puzzle is setting goals. People who know me personally or have worked with me know that I'm a big fan of goals. My life and work have provided me with enough evidence to confirm that human beings are capable of far more than we can even imagine.

But in order to tap into our limitless potential, we have to know what it is we want to accomplish. Setting goals is an important practice for creating a meaningful, satisfying, and successful life. And while the practice of goalsetting, in general, is important, there are certain ways to set goals that further increase the likelihood of success.

Motivational coach Zig Ziglar reminds us that "a goal properly set is halfway reached." Setting a goal is just like assembling a puzzle. Piece by piece, piece by piece, you make possible what at first seemed impossible. You get a little bit closer to living your best life. You've got what it takes. Continue to read this book and I will coach you on how to assemble the puzzle of your dream.

* * *

MICROPRODUCTI VITY IS THE TINY HABIT THAT WILL LEAD YOU TO HUGE WINS

"If you have enough reasons in life, anything is possible," Jim Rohn

Have you heard sentiments like these before? Of course, you have—breaking projects down into their component parts is oft-repeated advice when you're tackling something big. It's a principle that I call "microproductivity."

We think it's a term that perfectly captures the essence of this tried-and-true wisdom. It's way easier (not to mention far less overwhelming) to focus on putting one foot in front of the other —rather than gazing with dread at the entire marathon route ahead of you.

Breaking tasks down helps us to see large tasks as more approachable and doable, and reduces our propensity to procrastinate or defer tasks because we simply don't know where to begin.

That makes sense, right? But, here's the thing: Have you ever stopped to ask yourself *why* this tactic works? In the end, you're doing roughly the same amount of work. So, what exactly makes this "one puzzle at a time" strategy so helpful for all of us?

Let's dig into all of the science and psychology to identify the reasons behind why we all prefer dining on a "huge puzzle" just one fork-full at a time.

* * *

THE HUMAN
BRAIN IS LIMITED

Yes, our memory is flawed and limited. We can't remember everything. We all know this.

While memory limits can vary slightly from person to person, recent studies show that our average working memory capacity (working memory is what's used in mental tasks) is only three to five items. Anything more than that is bound to fall out of your brain.

If we rely on our memory, we'll stop at every step of the task and think, 'What am I supposed to do next? And those stops are opportunities to get distracted, get off track, or miss a step.

So, put simply, breaking a larger project down into smaller to-dos helps us easily identify what step we should take next. But there's one more important note to make about this: this process shouldn't happen mentally (because, in case you already forgot, your memory isn't all that great).

These individual steps should be physically written down on your task list on a digital board or in a checklist on your phone, for example. You can refer back to that as your roadmap for your project when you can't remember what comes next.

* * *

OUR WORK BETTER WITH SPECIFIC GOALS

You have a major goal in your mind—for example, you're spearheading the launch of an entirely new product for your organization.

At first glance, your goal seems simple: Get the new product ready. But, in reality, that's a pretty vague objective. When does it need to go live What qualifies as "ready"? How will you make this happen? Getting the entire product completed provides very little direction.

This is precisely why specificity is one of the core elements of the Goal-Setting Theory, established by psychologist Edwin Locke in the late 1960s.

In an article about the Goal-Setting Theory published in the Oxford Research Encyclopedia of Psychology, author and professor of Organizational Effectiveness, Gary Latham, cites four main reasons why specific goals are so powerful:

- Specific goals force us to make a choice to pursue them—and, as a result, exclude anything irrelevant. This increases our focus, as well as our sense of purpose in pursuing that goal.
- Similarly, specific goals incite effort, which is another cornerstone of motivation.
- Specific goals inspire us to be more persistent, as we have a clear idea of what success looks like.
- Specific goals immediately get our wheels turning on the strategies necessary to attain them.

Of course, there's plenty of other research that shows we tend to do better with specific goals. In just one study of 162 undergraduate students who were asked to perform a computerized hand-eye coordination test, researchers found a correlation between goal specificity and level of performance. They found that if one controlled for goal difficulty, setting specific personal goals resulted in higher levels of productivity.

Okay, but how does all of this tie back to the concept of microproductivity? Well, breaking a large project down into bite-sized tasks allows you to set far more specific milestones (i.e. "write the product description by the end of the day") and, as a result, keeps you motivated and moving in the right direction.

* * *

REGULAR FEEDBACK KEEPS YOU ON TRACK

Bigger projects can span weeks—sometimes even months or years. Can you think of anything more frustrating than investing all of that work into a task, only to discover at a much later date that you're totally off track?

This is another reason why breaking down these large assignments into smaller puzzles is so crucial: You have the opportunity to see retrospectives (which is another core tenet of the Agile methodology), receive feedback, and make adjustments when necessary.

In short, breaking a large project down into smaller tasks allows you to get feedback, make course corrections, and stay motivated toward the completion of it.

It's easy to think of feedback as demotivating, particularly when it's harsh or constructive. However, science proves that feedback of any type—whether it's positive or negative—inspires us to keep moving forward.

In a study of 157 participants who played a brain-training game, it was discovered that:

- Negative feedback decreased feelings of competence but still increased immediate game play.
- Negative feedback motivated participants to repair their short-term performance.
- Positive feedback fostered longer-term motivation in the participants.

So this shows that, perhaps surprisingly, both positive and negative feedback is helpful in terms of making adjustments and staying committed to the task at hand. And, that's something that you'll be missing if you try to tackle an entire goal in one fell swoop.

* * *

WE HATE WAITING FOR RESULTS

As humans, we're not excellent at delayed gratification. We like to see progress, and we like to see progress quickly and often.

You're probably familiar with that satisfied rush you get when you're able to cross something off your to-do list. But, what's happening in your brain when you check that box or scribble out that task? Well, your brain releases dopamine—a neurotransmitter that's connected to feelings of pleasure and motivation.

Here's the thing: You like the way that feels, so you'll make your best attempt to repeat that success. It's something that neuroscientists call "self-directed learning," and it's a big reason why splitting up large projects is so helpful.

By breaking those long-term assignments down, you open the door to experiencing more frequent rewards (and dopamine rushes), which inspire you to keep taking steps forward.

But you're wasting opportunities for an adrenaline rush by making a task too big. We are working with our own desires for reward and feedback by breaking a large task down into its component parts.

* * *

LET'S BREAK IT DOWN NOW

We all know by now that productivity is personal —what works well for one person might backfire for another. However, when it comes to feeling intimidated by large, daunting projects, the concept of segmenting that assignment into smaller goals is about as universally-helpful as a productivity tip can get.

There are certain characteristics of how humans think and work that are common. Breaking down a large task is very useful for people who are feeling overwhelmed or are not making progress on their projects and tasks.

The only thing left for you to do? Take that major goal (you know, the one you've been continuously pushing to the back burner), split it up into individual tasks, and get to work. No, you might not assemble that proverbial puzzle all in one sitting. But, honestly, why would you need to?

In order to do this, you have to keep it as simple as possible. All you need are goals and microtasks. Here is one example of how to split the big yearly goal into achievable microtasks:

Yearly Goal:

1. Start to learn the Ukrainian language and get a B1 certificate by the end of the year

Microtasks:

- Pass an initial test to identify my current Ukrainian language level
- Buy Ukrainian alphabet
- Find a teacher
- Take one lesson every week
- Listen to Ukrainian songs every day
- Start to watch cartoons in the Ukrainian language
- Pass pre-test
- Join Ukrainian speaking club
- Read a Ukrainian book
- Pass a test

Microproductivity is the micro version of the to-do

list. "One puzzle at a time" is scientifically proven to help you get more done step by step.

* * *

HOW TO SET, PLAN, AND PURSUE YOUR GREATEST GOALS

"Whatever the mind can conceive and believe the mind can achieve," Napoleon Hill

Aspiring to be greater than the person you are today is the best way to push yourself in the direction you want to go. Sitting down and outlining your life's goals will put you on the fast track toward life's success.

But how do you actually achieve your goals? What do you define as success? And what happens when you change your mind?

* * *

GET INSPIRED

Finding the inspiration for any endeavor in life is the essential first step, and it's often the hardest. A stroke of genius can happen at any moment, and it can propel you to achieve in places you never knew were possible. I advise starting with what you already have and know.

***

UNDERSTAND WHY

It's common to get caught up in the day-to-day tasks of what you're trying to achieve, and thus it's easy to lose sight of the greater purpose of why you're doing something at all.

Very often we just get busy. We don't take the time to sit back and evaluate progress. We're constantly evaluating metrics and analytics, but sometimes that's not the ultimate measure that we should be focused on. Taking a step back further to understand what you want out of life on a personal level can help inform you about which direction you ought to go.

That's why I spend some time reviewing my Yearly Goals. It's there that I can see what I have accomplished since last reviewed it, and also see where I got off track. I suggest you review your yearly goals right now. Don't have it? No stress! Read the next step.

* * *

MAKE A PLAN

Getting down your goals is the first step to empowering yourself. Writing them down and being able to reference them is a way to keep them slipping from your field of view.

Let's write your yearly goals right now. Just take a pen and paper and write down 10 real goals (no more for the beginning) you want to achieve by the end of this year in the positive present tense. Having positive present-tense goals programs the subconscious mind and builds faith and conviction inside you, that the goal is realizable. The way you accomplish this is by writing and re-writing your goals, having the ability to carry them with you, and reviewing them daily.

I also recommend you set up a detailed digital board (Trello for example) and make cards for each of your goals. It will help you to see the bigger picture and in this way, your life roadmap will be presented visually.

* * *

RECOGNIZE STRENGTHS AND WEAKNESSES

When it comes to knowing areas in which you excel, as well as where you don't, be honest with yourself and be realistic when setting goals.

I love tennis, but unfortunately, I'm not good enough to try to become a professional tennis player. As much as I'd like to dream that I could, that's just not a realistic thing to put on my goal list. There are certain things in life that you enjoy doing and are fun, but are okay to just keep as side hobbies.

The greater point here is to understand areas where you are strong and continue to refine those skills. Also, be honest with yourself about where you struggle and surround yourself with people who pick you up when you fall.

* * *

CONSTANTLY IMPROVE

There's always an element of surprise and transition in life. So even if you know *why* you're doing something, it's still important to recognize the need to constantly refine it and get better.

I am an avid reader of self-help books and listen to motivational speakers, old and new, to inspire me and give me a fresh perspective.

Even the very act of pushing yourself to learn more has improved over time.

Ultimately, everyone is looking to be more productive. Mapping out life goals can help you to gain a greater perspective on what's really important, as well as what is the most effective use of your time.

Have you started mapping out your life goals? Tell me what works for you, and how you've implemented those plans in your daily life. Find me on LinkedIn, Facebook, Instagram, or Twitter, and share your thoughts with me.

* * *

HOW TO MAKE YOUR GOALS ACHIEVABLE WITH THE SMART METHOD

A particularly powerful method of goal-setting uses the clever acronym SMART to guide the process of turning big dreams into reality. Once you've come up with a goal, check to be sure it meets SMART criteria:

Specific

Be clear and concrete about what you want to accomplish. It's much easier to work toward a specific goal (write 1,000 words per day) than it is to work toward a vague one (write a book). When working on this aspect of your goal, visualize what you and what your life will look like once you've accomplished it. That will help you to define exactly what you want to achieve.

Measurable

Set a goal that allows you to measure your progress toward achieving it. Ask yourself the following question: How will I know that I've accomplished my goal? First of all, it would be helpful to break the main goal down into small, measurable puzzles.

For example, if your main goal is to write a book, you can break that down into all the progressive puzzles you'll take along the way: Create a book name, write a manuscript, choose a cover, etc. Making your goal measurable is an important way to keep yourself on track. The bonus is that you can celebrate along the way as you attain each of the puzzles that bring you closer to success!

Attainable

Make your goals realistic. One of the biggest pitfalls

to success is making the goal too big. You don't want to bite off more than you can chew, so take some time to think carefully about your goal and be sure it's reasonable and realistic. If you're in your mid-40s and have a passion for football, it'll make much more sense to set a goal of becoming an amateur player than aiming to become a star player. Improve your chances of making your dreams come true by factoring reality into your plans.

Relevant

Set a goal that means something to you. Working toward your goals, no matter how big or small takes work. By setting a goal that you're passionate about and truly want to achieve, you'll be more likely to stay motivated along the way. When the going gets tough, you can remind yourself of how much you want to reach the finish of life and find the energy to keep going.

Time-Bound

Set a deadline, and commit to it! Putting time stamps on your goals is a way of holding yourself accountable and making sure you stay focused and on task. You may need to do some research to find out how long you can reasonably expect to have to work on your goal before you can accomplish it. If you don't set a deadline, you won't be nearly as likely to stay committed and keep the wheels in motion.

Check-in with your deadline every now and again to be sure it remains realistic, and use it as a way to stay motivated.

* * *

HOW TO TRAIN YOUR BRAIN TO BE MORE PRODUCTIVE WITH MICROTASKS

"Productivity is being able to do things that you were never able to do before," Franz Kafka

Is there anything more satisfying than completing a long checklist of small tasks? The simple act of crossing off items on your to-do list is a blissful feeling.

Whether you're supermotivated or hyperactive, we all need checklists to keep track of our many professional and passion goals—especially when they involve several moving parts and multiple team members.

If you think you're the only one who feels a sense of accomplishment and satisfaction after checking that last box on the list, think again! All my product teams and clients use digital checklists to track the progress of short and long-term projects. And we get pretty excited when that little green icon shows up on the project's card because it means we've finished all the items on our lengthy list and the project is done.

Accomplishing microtasks is more than a cause for celebration. There's a reason why we get excited over this sense of success. Let's explore these simple, yet powerful psychological motivators.

* * *

THE POWER OF MICROTASKS

As we discussed in previous chapters, big goals are important. They give us something to work towards. But microtasks are important, too. Once an overarching goal has been established ("Let's work on increasing subscribers to our social media webpage," for example), it's time to set small, achievable tasks for everyone.

Use the SMART approach as a guiding light to organizing big goals. Meantime, checklists should be made up of small, actionable microtasks that feel doable to the individuals and teams working to complete them.

Microtasks are inherently short-term, which is beneficial when trying to accomplish big goals. Bigger goals usually take some time: they tend to be complicated and require patience. It's common for people to get frustrated when the process takes longer than they were expecting, which is a big reason why people give up mid-project.

Breaking down your goals into smaller, microtasks help you stay motivated and positive throughout the process.

* * *

WHAT'S GOING ON IN OUR BRAINS? MOTIVATION!

Motivation is an essential and irreplaceable element of success. When we're not motivated, we fail. Haven't we all felt that mid-task slump?

When we experience even small amounts of success, our brains release dopamine, which is connected to feelings of pleasure, learning, and *motivation*. When we feel the effects of dopamine, we're eager to repeat the actions that resulted in that success in the first place. Neuroscientists refer to this as "self-directed learning."

When we are positively motivated to do something,

we learn to take that same action to receive the same feeling. This is why achieving small tasks is such an effective way to stay motivated during long-term projects and processes.

Checking microtasks off of a checklist releases small amounts of dopamine that then fuel us to keep checking off more items, i.e. get more done. Raise your hand if you've ever written a task down just to immediately check it off.

But at the same time checklist items have to be actual, substantial small tasks to be effective in actually accomplishing your to-do list or getting closer to the project end date.

* * *

SLICE AND DICE YOUR BIG GOALS WITH EXCITEMENT

I can pretty much guarantee that you've all experienced gamification at some point, even if you're not familiar with the term.

It's a process that takes normal, mundane tasks and turns them into "fun" activities with elements like competition and rewards systems. This idea is used by many industries, fields, and platforms that may surprise you, and one example of this idea in practice is a checklist with microtasks.

When working on a checklist, you complete actions and tasks to receive a type of reward. While not in the traditional sense, a completed project and completed checklist are both examples of something our brain would view as "rewards."

Think about your smartphone. If you have a pedometer app, you might earn a golden ribbon for completing your step goal that day. In the same line of thought, some digital checklist gives you a green, completed icon whenever a checklist's item is finished.

These rewards might seem a little trite, but our brains respond to satisfying markers of success like this—and push us to achieve more because of it. A crucial aspect of gamification, however, is that the rewards given must actually be earned. This isn't because of any honor system amongst colleagues. It's because people can sense when they haven't really earned a reward, and this feeling makes the reward seem less meaningful.

If the tasks on your checklist are unchallenging, the result will be unsatisfying. Triggering the dopamine response requires some sincere effort. So while I did say that microtasks are more effective than large ones, they must be big enough so you experience at least some sense of satisfaction and pride in completing them. For example, emptying the washing machine every day is an accomplishment, but may not give you the same feeling of satisfaction as finishing the first step of the programming process.

* * *

MICROTASKS FOR EVERYTHING

People use checklists for all sorts of things: keeping track of homework assignments, onboarding a new hire, packing for vacation, or organizing their book collections. The possibilities are truly endless. And checklists can be *especially* useful in a professional setting when dealing with highly complicated goals.

For example, my teams use a checklist feature to mark progress on long-term production pieces like microphones. With microphones, the actual writing of the checklist is very important. We have several departments working on several different aspects of the project and shared digital checklists are the perfect way to manage this workflow.

Each one of the checklist's items presents its own unique obstacles that must be tackled. Checking an item off of the list is immensely satisfying for everyone involved and then it's on to the next item.

Workflows like this apply to your personal life too. All it takes is some time to slice your big goals into achievable microtasks. You should also spend a little time once per month to evaluate progress as well as celebrate your successes. That's all!

* * *

IT'S YOUR TIME TO ACCOMPLISH SOME MICROTASKS

By understanding the psychological reasons and motivators, our love for completed checklist items makes complete sense. Not only does a completed task signify that you are one step closer to your dream—but it also means that you accomplished something real and meaningful. Each checklist item was a challenge (large or small) that you overcame.

So the next time you feel amazing after checking all the microtasks off of your goals checklist, you'll know exactly why. Keep on making those lists. Microproductivity rock!

* * *

APPLY MICRO HABITS ELSEWHERE

"Formal education will make you a living, but self-education will make you a fortune," Jim Rohn

Micro Habits is more than just a strategy to teach you how to develop healthy new habits—it's a guide for self-awareness. Use micro habits techniques for any area of your life in which you want to take action. The better you get at micro habits, the more success you'll have in all areas of your life. I wish you a very exciting Micro Habits journey and micro successes, but over and over and over again.

* * *

FINAL NOTE

If you believe this book shares an important message, please leave a review on Amazon. Reviews (in quantity and in rating) are the main metric people use to judge a book's content. And if you have great results with micro habits, please come back and tell other readers (and me) about your success! Every single review has a huge impact on others' willingness to read a book, and if this changes your life, you can change someone else's life by spreading the word.

WHAT SHOULD YOU READ NEXT?

Thank you so much for taking the time to read this book. It has been a pleasure sharing my work with you. If you are looking for something to read next, allow me to offer a suggestion. Below you can find a list of book series also written by me and I believe you will find them interesting. (This list was updated on February 2023, for the latest updates check on Amazon.)

5 STEPS

The 1st Simple Step to Your Perfect Home: How to Methodologically Sort Through All Items, Keep Important, and Get Rid of Unnecessary

The 2nd Simple Step to Your Perfect Home: How to Methodically Put All Necessary Items in the Optimal

MINDFUL MOMENTS COLLECTION

The Mindful Thrift: How to Appreciate What We Have and Save What We Do Not Notice

The Mindful Nutrition: How to Enjoy the True Taste of Food, Have a Slim Body and 33 (+3) Home Cooking Recipes for a Delicious Degustation

The Mindful Eating for Beginners: Step-by-Step Guide for Lifelong Health and Collection of Quick & Easy Recipes for Every Day

ACKNOWLEDGMENTS

I want to thank my family who supports me on my writing journey. Also, I want to thank all the professionals who helped me publish my work. Finally, I want to thank you, dear reader, for choosing this book from among the millions existing. It's truly inspiring!

NOTES

«Lally, P., C. H. M. van Jaarsveld, H. W. W. Potts, & J. Wardle. How are habits formed: Modelling habit formation in the real world. Eur. J. Soc. Psychol., (2010). v 40, 998–1009. doi: 10.1002/ejsp.674»

«Knowlton, B J, J. A Mangels, and L. R. Squire. A Neostriatal Habit Learning System in Humans. Science 273, (1996). n 5280, 1399»

«Wood, W., J. M. Quinn, & D. A. Kashy. Habits in everyday life: Thought, emotion, and action. Journal of Personality and Social Psychology. (Dec 2002). v 83(6), 1281-1297.»